I0421641

Why Are They Like That? Rich and Poor

*Questions you've dared to ask, answered
by real people, celebrities and experts*

A book series based on the award-winning
sharing project that's captured worldwide
attention helping people in their personal,
social and business relationships

Phillip J. Milano

For Robin, Jacob, Lucas and Ben

Publisher:
Y Forum
yforum@yforum.com

ISBN: 978-1-07-956212-5

Cover and interior layout by Sandy Weber,
Key 3 Creative, Jacksonville, Florida
Cover photo credit: Rawpixel. Stock photo for illustrative purposes
only; any person depicted is a posed model.

Content based in part on the popular Y? sharing project and Dare
to Ask column

Find out more about the author, upcoming books and speeches at
www.phillipmilano.com, www.facebook.com/PhillipJMilano or
@PhillipMilano.

Books In This Series

Why Are They Like That? Blacks

Why Are They Like That? Whites

Why Are They Like That? Hispanics

Why Are They Like That? Asians

Why Are They Like That? Gay Men

Why Are They Like That? Lesbians

Why Are They Like That? Women

Why Are They Like That? Men

Why Are They Like That? Rich and Poor

Why Are They Like That? Religious (or not)

Why Are They Like That? Disabled People

Why Are They Like That? Young and Old

Praise for the Y? sharing project and the book "I Can't Believe You Asked That!" (Perigee)

"Milano is quietly revolutionizing cross-cultural communication..."
- *Pulitzer Prize-winning columnist Leonard Pitts*

"If you've ever hesitated to ask a question because you think it might be considered insensitive or impolitic, now is your chance ... Nothing is considered out of bounds..."
- *CNN Headline News*

"(It) tells more about who we are and how we feel about each other than you're likely to learn from a dozen sociology texts…"
- *Washington Post News Service*

"Mr. Milano has dared to open the field of debate to the maximum…"
- *Le Monde, Paris*

"(A) remarkable contribution to cross-cultural understanding…"
- *The (London) Guardian*

"A truly rare achievement ... has the potential to have a profound impact on the way we all see and understand each other..."
- *Playboy magazine*

"It's an incredible book. It diffuses everything ... Nothing is off limits, and the questions have that childlike honesty to them..."
- *Dee Snider, Twisted Sister; host, "Dee Snider Radio"*

"A take-no-prisoners attitude prevails between the volume's covers . . . This book is hard to put down..."
- *Midwest Book Review*

"A+ (highest rating) ... Everything you wanted to know but were afraid to ask gets tackled here ..."
- *Entertainment Weekly*

4

CONTENTS

Introduction

Why Are They Like That? is a series of books based on an award-winning worldwide sharing project in which real people, experts and celebrities talk about things that make us different from each other. Silly things. Sad things. Funny things. Profound things.

Read with an open mind and we believe that by the time you're finished you'll have a much better understanding of how to make more and real friends, money and love. It's that simple.

Why? Because this isn't about trying to get ahead with diversity training. We are well beyond that. According to the Census Bureau, by 2050 the United States will have no racial or ethnic minority.

No, this is about moving past talking about how to understand each other to talking to each other. Right now.

That's why there's no agenda to these books other than getting the conversation going. We can discuss studies and methods for elevating social consciousness all we want, but there is no substitute for real dialogue.

That's where Why Are They Like That? stands apart from other books on the topic. You will see how people talk about their real differences of race, religion, sex, disability and more.

The success of the approach is proven: It's based on the ground-breaking Y? website project, blog and column that have attracted millions of visitors and worldwide media attention.

Our hope is that by reading, you will become more comfortable asking and answering the questions yourself, expecting the unexpected in return and helping change the ground rules for how we learn from and about each other. To that end, we wrap up each book in the series with our O.U.T.L.O.U.D. Method for Dialogue, with tips to help you get your own conversations started. Ultimately, that is what this effort is all about.

After all, if you want to make more friends, money and love, you better know the people you're talking to, selling to or opening to. Knowledge isn't just power. It's all power.

Enjoy.

Phillip J. Milano
Founder, Y?

Do cops turn up the heat in tough areas?

They asked:

I grew up in a middle-class community, and when I encountered police, they were always polite and friendly. Later I lived in a poor area. I saw police often, and in interactions with them, even the most innocuous, they were consistently insulting and threatening. I'd like to ask law enforcement officers to explain this difference in attitude.

Laura, 37, Baltimore

You said:

When I patrolled in a mostly blue-collar urban environment, I "lowered" my vocabulary and mannerisms. A police officer must often get people to do things they ordinarily would not. If I want a subject to stop, turn and place his hands on his head, I don't want that lost in translation. If he balks, my voice and mannerisms will become more demonstrative and generally include foul language. This usually works because the person respects strength. "Sir, please stop walking and place your hands on your head" is an invitation to violence.

M.D., 32, Houston

Unfortunately, police ... have fears and prejudices based on their experiences in a given environment. They perceive the threat of their surroundings in much the same way you might. Do you behave in the same manner in a community with drugs and violence that you do in a white suburb?

Dee, 46, male, Detroit

There are more "bad" people in poorer neighborhoods. They are hostile to all types of authority. Most do not respect or respond to cops unless the cop swears or does something else to establish his authority.

Anonymous, Michigan

We found:

Yes, police are more threatening and aggressive in poorer, high-crime areas, according to years of studies of citizen complaints and police officers' own reports.

Policing expert Wesley Skogan (skogan.org), professor in Northwestern University's Institute for Policy Research and author of such books as "Community Policing: Can It Work?" and "Police and Community in Chicago," said cops want to gain the upper hand from the get-go.

"If police perceive danger to self or being unable to control an interaction, they feel they must be aggressive right out of the box," he said. "They want the public always responding to them, not the other way around."

A prime goal is to get compliance rapidly before a crowd gathers.

"If a crowd starts yelling, they won't be silent. So you want to move it along quickly," he said. "I'm not saying it's the smartest or right thing."

There are often better ways to manage encounters, training shows.

"Show a little respect, let the person retain a shred of dignity — instead of 'Shut your mouth motherfucker and up against the wall,' " Skogan said.

The problem is that rookies, often assigned the nastier beats in town, hear veterans' tales and assume a threatening style works best in certain situations, he said. But research shows verbal abuse or unsnapping a gun's holster just create more suspicion and lack of trust.

"Be firm but professional," he said. "And don't pretend to talk the language of the street."

Are urine for an icy surprise at spiffy restaurants?

They asked:

Why do urinals in fancy restaurants have ice in them?

Paul P, white, middle class, Jacksonville

You said:

I always assumed it was an attempt to reduce odors in a classier way than using a perfumed urinal cake.

Jerry, 61, New Britain, Conn.

So if you don't flush, the hot urine will melt the ice and kinda flush it for you. If you don't flush a urinal, the salt in your urine will build up and clog the pipes.

Mark, Michigan

It is thought that it keeps the stink down.

Wendi, Philadelphia

Mostly due to dropped ice or when people in restaurants claim they have something in their glass they dump the remains there. They aren't supposed to but depending on your server and their attitude you might not worry about it and take care of business.

Bruce, 49, Newark, N.J.

We found:

If we only knew what the seemingly pissy guy from Jersey was trying to say, all would be well with our waterworld.

Public urinal deodorizing is a complicated thing. Paradichlorobenzene-free urinal cakes? Waterless no-flush? Sanor System ("Clean Restrooms, Happy People")? Plain old ice chips? We shudder at the choices. And since chap who asked us this probably didn't want to go Googling it at work, there we were to provide comfort and sanitation — er, sanity.

10

Turns out icy urinals aren't a hallmark of expensive hotels and restaurants, but of old ones, said Kevin Moll, founder and CEO of Denver-based National Restaurant Consultants (restaurantconsulting.us), which offers wisdom to the hospitality industry.

"With the sewer lines in older hotels, because they're so long, a foul odor can permeate up through the pipes, so ... if you keep ice in there, or even just water, it keeps the odor away. The melting ice creates a constant drip, enough to keep it away."

Older hotels or eateries may still use iron pipes, too, and when iron and urine mix, it's nothing to sniff at.

"The newer places have PVC pipe, so it's rare to find ice in their urinals," Moll said. "In older places if there's no water or ice, the acidic urine hits the iron and can create a smell."

Sit-down toilets have water in them, so ladies' rooms don't need ice, he added.

Since we're talking, what's in those fancy bathrooms that are off-limits to we of the proletariat, anyway?

A quick list from Moll, and then we really have to go:

Expensive hand lotion and French-milled soap, mouthwash, breath mints, all-linen towels, a seating area, top-of-the-line sink and water closet hardware, bidets and, in some off-the-chain cases, clear-glass stall doors and walls that miraculously fog up upon closing the door. Now that's going in style.

Oh, and, of course, a concierge to make you feel all special inside.

"Excellent restrooms are extremely important to a place's success," Moll said. "If it's important to the top management, it will trickle down — just like the ice."

Are the People of Walmart different from the People of Target?

They asked:

At our local stores there is a huge difference in the type of people who shop in Walmart compared to Target. Are the Walmarts in other areas like this?

Trent, Fargo, N.D.

You said:

I don't understand the need for many Walmart customers who seem to make an effort to be offensive and walk around with a "Kiss My Ass" attitude.

Joyce, white, Middleburg

Walmart generally appeals to a broader class of people, including the lower classes. Targets tend to have merchandise designed to cater to the budget-minded middle and upper classes.

Kristy, 30, white female, Albany, Ga.

I find nicer products at Target and an overall less-trashy feel from the store condition and shoppers.

Scott, white, Ohio

We found:

We're going to get to the too-tight clothes and insane hair stuff. Have patience. But let us at least create the appearance of propriety by first discussing some findings by consumer shopping analyst Scarborough Research:

— Target-exclusive shoppers are more likely to be female, younger and richer. For example, Target-exclusives have an average household income of about $85,000, compared to $57,000 for Walmart-exclusives, according to one survey.

— Walmart-exclusives are most likely to also be in the checkout lanes at Dollar General, Family Dollar and Big Lots, while Target-exclusives are hitting up Nordstrom, Macy's, Costco and Mervyn's.

— Walmart is big in smaller and Southern markets, while Target performs best in larger urban areas.

But enough of that. Why does it seem so many more people sport jaw-dropping hairstyles and expose their butt cracks at Wally-World?

"There does seem to be a lot hanging out where there shouldn't be," said PeopleofWalmart.com co-founder Luke Wherry. The site, which gets millions of visitors monthly, posts hilarious submitted photos of Walmart customers. (Visit it. Oh, you already have.)

But Wherry, who shops both Walmart and Target, said the site isn't poking fun at the poor.

"Some of these customers could be wealthy, but they are wearing ridiculous stuff. ... We are just portraying Americans and their poor fashion choices."

Wherry said while Target has its share of customers who seem above ever stepping inside a Walmart, Walmart just attracts, well, everyone, from low-incomers to Ferrari owners. So naturally, you might see strange goings-on more frequently there.

More people – regular, God-fearing folks – just seem to pop into Walmart on a bad day, and if they do, chances are they might wind up on PeopleofWalmart.com, said Wherry.

In addition to odd garb, Walmart shoppers love to bring in animals like skunks and stuff, including someone once accompanied by a mini-horse. Wherry's personal favorite?

The photo captioned "Need More Supplies," of a guy sporting a red tie-dyed shirt and face covered in gold spray paint, and the only thing in his cart seems to be gold spray paint.

"Obviously a huffer."

Hungry? Just buy a Whopper and move on

They asked:

Why is there so much attention paid to campaigns to feed the hungry? Who can be hungry in America when you can get a hamburger for less than a dollar?

Mike, 63, Sarasota

You said:

If you're that out of touch, you should go to work in D.C. You'd fit right in.

Donald, St. Augustine

I've been in the position where I had to choose between buying groceries or paying rent. I paid the rent and went without food. Many have to make that choice for much longer periods of time. Some are too proud to ask for help, and some, like me, don't qualify but still don't have the wherewithal to buy food. Going hungry has serious long-term health repercussions, so if you have the resources, it's appreciated if you help those who don't.

Robin, 55, female, Westland, Mich.

I work with low-income and homeless families struggling each day to feed their families. We have many families struggling to keep a roof over their heads, and after paying electric and water, there isn't much left for food ... There is no $1 for a hamburger, and the number of hungry children and families is growing.

Debi, St. Johns County

We found:

It might be fun for a little while to buy cheap burgers all the time to fill yourself up. You could be like Morgan Spurlock in the "Super Size Me" documentary, who did it for 30 days straight, got seriously ill and even hurled in a McDonald's parking lot. He got a reality TV show, which is everything.

"It's possible for $5 a day to fill your belly, say with white bread, but you and your family would get sick and run up health costs. ... And your kids would do crappy in school," said Jim Weill, president of the non-profit Food Research and Action Center (frac.org) in Washington, which works to eradicate hunger. "Same with cheeseburgers. You can fill up for small amounts of money, but you can't function in society unless you get a minimally adequate diet."

And that's assuming you even have enough money for burgers.

About 11 percent of the American population lives near the edge of hunger, according to the U.S. Department of Agriculture. That's about 38 million people, 14 million of them children.

It's called "food insecurity," Weill said: not having enough resources for a minimally healthful, adequate diet.

Either that, or people eat a lousy diet of cheap, high-calorie food. Or, he said, parents do things like cut their kids' milk with water to keep their bellies full. Or, the parents feed their kids and go hungry themselves.

Still, some people wonder why hungry folks own TVs, forgetting that the TV may have been bought before losing a job, he said.

"Some people, I think, may see campaigns about hunger as inappropriate efforts to improve government programs," Weill said. "But families still need enough resources to participate in the mainstream economy."

Wealth isn't a license for rudeness

They asked:

I always figured the higher someone's education and the more money, the better their manners. So why do so many people with money and education seem to be the rudest?

G. Havill, 19, female, Mount Vernon, Iowa

You said:

Sometimes people with a lot of money or with a lot of education seem to think they are "better" than others. But "more" does not always make something "better."

S. Rollison, 49, female, New Alexandria, Pa.

It's a matter of training, not money, and an increasing number of people who have the latter disdain the former as "beneath them." "Upper class" and "classy" are pretty much a contradiction in terms.

Ann, 40, Kansas City, Mo.

It may have to do with centuries of cocky, mean upper-class gentry types from past civilizations. . . . The other theory is that poor people are more generous because they know what it's like to be poor.

Stephanie, Washington, D.C.

We found:

We thought we'd get at least a few "they're just like the rest of us, no better and no worse"-type responses. Where's the love?

We found a whiz who studied the wealthy, and yep, he found that they're just like the rest of us, no better and no worse.

Most people think rich folks inherited their money or got it by an unfair advantage, but that's usually not the case, said Doug Harrison, co-author of "The New Elite: Inside the Minds of the Truly Wealthy."

16

For example, about 90 percent of the wealth earned in the United States in the past decade was by entrepreneurs from the middle class who worked their way up the hard way, he said.

"People who created wealth usually have good values," said Harrison, who with his co-authors talked to about 4,000 people across the top 10 percent of the U.S. economy, "with a serious focus on people with $5 million or greater in liquidity."

"You don't become successful by being a jerk, you do it by being good to people who work for you and to your customers and your bankers."

The problem is, many of us don't know it when we encounter rich types, most of whom are "regular people," so we don't "see" behavior that counters media stereotypes of "stupid, flippant" richies such as Paris Hilton or Britney Spears, he said.

Plus, maybe poorer people's nastiness gets a free pass because they don't have an advantage over you.

"If you run into rude rich people, you might be like 'God they are an asshole. If I was in that position I wouldn't be that way,' but if it's a rude redneck, you might think 'Well of course they're going to be that way, and I don't care because I'm better than them.' "

Not all upper-crusts are perfect, though.

"Some have people around them who allow them to be very efficient, so they get used to it," Harrison said. "They start expecting it, so if someone fails to perform, it can tick them off."

Low-income parents not into getting schooled

They asked:

I teach in a low- to middle- class area and want to know why some parents seem to put little value on their children's education. It kills me to see this happening to kids before they know what they could be capable of.

Marita, 27, Athens, Ga.

You said:

My advice, as a psychologist, is find time for each parent outside the school. The building itself is enough to spring instant walls for those who are afraid.

Jon, 33, Pepin, Wis.

I was raised by a single mother from a poor neighborhood. She emphasized the importance of education, even though she never attended beyond high school.

SoulOnIce, 26, male, Philadelphia

A lot of parents look down on education because they don't see how exactly it can help their kids be better off.

Ryan, 20, Dallas

Some lower-class parents may believe "What's good enough for me is good enough for my kids."

J.F., 24, female, Houston

This is a tired question. What if every minority in the U.S. got an education? Who would pick up the garbage or serve you your frappuccino at Starbucks?

Educated Latino, 26, male, Akron, Ohio

My parents came from Eastern Europe and valued education. Some North Americans have a disrespect for achievement.

A. Urbonas, Canada

We found:

A couple of concepts to consider here, said Patrick Finn (literacywithanattitude.com), associate professor emeritus of education at State University of New York at Buffalo, who wrote "Literacy with an Attitude: Educating Working-Class Children in Their Own Self-Interest."

– Some people, whether minority or poor, develop "oppositional identity" – a part of their identity forms in opposition to those they feel have basically shafted them. They may not respect those in authority, such as a teacher, and they may also act culturally opposite from the authority figure.

– Studies show that wealthier students are rewarded for being assertive and inquisitive, while classrooms of working-class students are rewarded for being docile and obedient. Using only traditional methods to reach lower-income students might bore them or cause them to feel they are being ordered around or held down.

"So the kid thinks, 'I'm tired of doing the 30th worksheet, I'm just tired of it,' " Finn said.

Some teachers are condescending to lower-income parents, while parents may feel they are being brought up to the school to be lectured – all at the same school they themselves attended and where they may have had bad experiences.

One solution: get teachers on board with progressive methods, while also bringing parents and teachers together to dialogue in workshops.

"With a frank conversation, the teacher may say, 'I never knew the parents were that concerned about the kids,' and the parents may say, 'I never realized the teachers were nice and doing the best they can.' "

He stocks up, and doesn't like the stares

They asked:

Why is it that when I buy foods in large quantities, people make rude comments like "how hungry" I must be, or "have a big crowd tonight?"

J.P., 36, male, Washington

You said:

People like to make small talk in grocery aisles thinking they're being "friendly." I once saw a cashier who was trying to be friendly: the very large man in front of me had a cart full of Lean Cuisine boxes. The cashier looked at the boxes and at the man and actually said, "I guess these aren't working."

Nikfish, 31, female, Canada

Some people probably assume you're just being piggish. Some people are always opening up their hole when they don't need to . . . you look at them and want to say, "Who the hell asked you, anyway?"

Monique, Fort Myers

A big part of it is that 75 percent of the population can't cook a meal that doesn't come in a box. It's unusual to see someone buying five chickens when it isn't the Fourth of July.

Brad, 32, Provo, Utah

I doubt most people are intentionally being rude. My guess is they are just teasing.

Matt, 20, Riverside, Calif.

When they look at you like you're a pig next time you go shopping, just think to yourself, "Hey, I am the smart one when I go shopping."

Melissa, 21, Grafton, N.D.

We make a day of going to Costco because it's fun, and why not save money and get all the toilet paper you'll need for a year?

Whitney, 20, Seattle

We found:

First, about people who stockpile:

Studies show about 80 percent of stockpiling is done by 20 percent of shoppers.

"Two things drive stockpiling, other than a sale: one is scarcity fear, and we see this motivating older people," said marketing professor Brian Wansink (mindlesseating.org), director of Cornell University's Food and Brand Lab and author of "Mindless Eating: Why We Eat More Than We Think."

"The second is a hoarding mentality, or over-planning. These are people who buy wrapping paper right after Christmas, for next year. Or people who go to Sam's and say I don't know what this is, but I need three . . ."

Now, about people who stare oddly at stockpilers:

"For some people, say younger people who are puzzled, a good analogy might be exercise, a long-horizon behavior: if you look at somebody who over-exercises, some might say, yeah, whatever, while a few say 'what a lunatic.' Only a small percentage of people might freak out at those who stockpile. These might be people who lead a more hedonic lifestyle, or who live for today."

And for those who do bulk-buy food: you might save on cost per unit, but it can be a pyrrhic victory if it goes stale, or, conversely, if you gobble it up too quickly.

"Research shows that virtually anything you buy in bulk, 50 percent tends to be eaten within six days of purchase," Wansink said. "If you want to get bulk savings, but you don't want to overeat, make sure you store it out of sight."

We trust that they wouldn't say no to these funds

They asked:

I keep hearing about affluent teenagers having "trust funds." What, may I ask, is a trust fund?

Lynda, 20, Bronx, N.Y.

You said:

Typically it's money set aside for a person for getting started in life, placed "in trust" so that it cannot be accessed until certain conditions are met, like turning 18/21, graduation of some kind, getting married, etc. I've never met anybody who had one that I knew about, but some people don't share that stuff as eagerly – it might make you look like a cream puff if others think you can't/don't have to make it on your own.

Chris, 37, Long Beach, Calif.

It is normally set up by a grandparent with restrictions on it like the grandchild has to be 25 before they can have the money, or it is only for school payments.

John, Salem, Va.

We found:

For people with trust funds (many of them are not reading this but have retained others to do so for them), it often is about protecting them from themselves, said Michael Silver, a CPA with Miami accounting firm Mallah Furman who has decades of experience with trust funds.

There are good reasons for this, he noted. For example, the parents may be wealthy, with a child in a high-risk profession, such as a physician, and may want to try to protect assets from claims of creditors in case of malpractice.

Then again, "You could have a worst-case scenario, say a drug addict [for a child], and you don't want them to get their hands on the money, so you put it in the hands of a trustee with some provisions dictating how the assets are distributed," he said.

Here's how all this might typically work: Your nice mom and dad have extra moolah, so they decide to become "grantors," setting aside some of said cabbage in a trust fund, which is overseen by a trustee, who holds title to the dinero for the sole benefit of very grateful you, the beneficiary. The trustee disperses the stacks according to the wishes of the grantor, which might mean you won't get any Benjamins until legit needs arise, like paying for college, owning a home or going on underwear-less drunken binges on Santa Monica Boulevard.

Some trusts are even set up as "spendthrift" trusts, according to Irv Blackman, a South Florida CPA who writes the "Tax Secrets of the Wealthy" newspaper column (taxsecretsofthewealthy.com). In that case, the trustee doesn't just oversee things but actually pays the beneficiary's bills because the child isn't good with money.

In reality, though, with many trusts, the money doesn't change a person's lifestyle, and the parents add requirements so their kids don't "lay back and not work," he said. "And often the kids will just leave it there in the trust until retirement."

Unless, that is, there is no trust fund, as with late hotelier Leona Helmsley, who left a $12 million trust to her dog but kept two grandkids out of the will.

What's with the hot "ghetto" mess?

They asked:

Why is it that whenever the media (or the show COPS) goes into a poor house/apartment, there is almost always a bare mattress on the floor and piles of clothes everywhere? I understand if one could not afford a box spring or dresser, but do you have to be so sloppy?

Bride, female, Detroit

You said:

When I was little, my parents divorced, and we moved into a little "ghetto" apartment. I shared a room with my sister, and we had a mattress on the ground. We always jumped on it and trashed the room every chance we got. My mom worked all day and took care of us when we weren't in day care. Her cleaning was taken up by basic things like keeping the kitchen and bathroom clean enough to keep us healthy; things like clothes on the ground could "go until next week."

Robin C., 20, Denver

The media purposefully make poor people look like lazy slobs.

Erika, 25, lower middle class, Portland, Maine

I just moved out of the second-poorest neighborhood in my city. It's the apathy that gets or keeps them in the slums, that leads to the slovenly lifestyle.

Jason, 30, Medford, Ore.

I grew up in a mobile home in Michigan. I am probably just like the people on COPS. But my apartment is really nice. I always have sheets on the bed. It isn't a reflection of the poor. It's just how they choose to live. I bet some places on COPS are middle-class, but they just don't choose to "look" that way. Probably for the same reasons they are on COPS: they are nuts!

Erin, 20, Anaheim, Calif.

We found:

It's not just the rich and non-criminal who keep a nice house. Frank McCann, director of Just Neighbors, a program of the New Jersey-based Family Promise help agency (familypromise.org) that shows people what it's like to be poor, said most often, those in poverty live in dignity.

"We need to examine the conditions under which people bring TV cameras in," said McCann, who's worked on poverty issues more than 30 years. "The landlord may not have cared for the building, or water may be leaking. That causes people to live differently.

"Also, it's usually an extraordinarily disrupted time when cameras visit. Yes, there may be clothes on the floor during a news event or disruption."

Mostly, a clean room with sheets on the bed has less to do with economics than with training, size and strength of a family, and time to devote to such chores, McCann said.

"Poorer people may not have the options we have, such as a cleaning lady. Despite that, most families in poor conditions don't live that way. They may not have the newest clothes or freshest paint, but they aren't living in slop and dirt."

Ultimately, learning proper living habits applies to poor and rich alike, McCann said.

"For that matter, I could take you to my son's room at Georgetown, and you'd see clothes on the floor. It has nothing to do with economics. Some people are organized; some aren't."

He says he works hard for the money

They asked:

I sold my business and am well-off. People think of me as "lucky" to be born white and smart, that my parents encouraged me, etc. But I worked hard to get where I am. Do people not as well-off think I am "just lucky," like someone who inherited wealth is?

J.D., 47, male, Summit, N.J.

You said:

As my mother would say: "People make their own luck."

Lee, 32, female, Los Angeles

Too many folks with wealth tell the half-truth that "hard work" got them where they are. Surely you know that the people who scrub your toilets work far harder than you ever did. Count your blessings . . .

JB, 32, female, Seattle

I spent most of my life on heroin and cocaine. . . . It was fun, really, fun – and now I'm going to one of the top 10 schools (because of who my dad is) in the country. I remember talking to my lawyer for my latest larceny charge, and she told me I had three things going for me: I was white, upper-middle class and young. Am I lucky? Yes. Proud? No. Would I trade my place with anyone? No.

Tommy, 22, Raleigh, N.C.

You have done what you needed to get where you are. I grew up as poor white trash. I decided I wanted out of that situation. Those who consider me lucky are victim wannabes.

Danny, 40, Atlanta

Danny: I don't loathe people who have done well, especially those reaping the rewards of working hard. But I am deeply concerned about the powerful influence of the super-wealthy and giant corporations.

Sarah M., 26, Portland, Ore.

We found:

Psychologist Richard Wiseman (richardwiseman.com) of the University of Hertfordshire in England is author of "The Luck Factor" and has spent years offering well-researched reasons why some people are lucky and others not.

To quote from his 2003 article in The Skeptical Inquirer: "Lucky people generate their own good fortune via four basic principles. They are skilled at creating and noticing chance opportunities, make lucky decisions by listening to their intuition, create self-fulfilling prophesies via positive expectations, and adopt a resilient attitude that transforms bad luck into good."

Shira Boss, author of "Green With Envy: Why Keeping Up with the Joneses is Keeping us in Debt" (greenwithenvythebook.com), said most people believe in the American dream: that no matter who you are, you can be successful.

"We see self-made people differently than those with inherited wealth, which we see as not fair."

The self-made don't get off too easily, though, she said.

"If you inherited wealth, that's at least an explanation. But the more you are like someone who 'made it,' the more it might bother you. Do we really want to say he was smarter? We'd rather say he was lucky."

Does all that money hide you from the real world?

They asked:

For middle-class to rich people: Do you feel you've missed out on the genuine experience of life by being sheltered by your money? And do you think poor people are more "real" than you?

Amber, lower class, Arkansas

You said:

Our loved ones can get killed, our children can do drugs and our lives can fall to pieces, just like yours.

Mary, 29, middle class, Philadelphia

As soon as my dad got a high-paying job, our family became torn apart. Lots of possessions and the greater living space caused envy, greed and fighting.

Brianna, Glendora, Calif.

I don't think I've missed out on anything. I think "close" poor families and "dysfunctional" wealthy families are stereotypes. I have a loving family and I can shop at Bloomingdale's.

Victoria, 15, upper class, Scranton, Pa.

Grandpa died a few years back and left me $30,000. I didn't worry about groceries, bought the piano I wanted, paid for college, but never got laid during this time. Been poor: living off credit cards and minimum wage, wondering how to pay for food, staying home 'cause of no money, and never got laid. Bottom line: rich is better ... and I don't get laid much.

Chris, 34, middle class, Va.

Poorer people are braver. I missed out on lighting candles in the house and calling it a candle party when you can't pay the electric bill, or going to the park instead of a movie because you can't afford a movie. We can't ever understand what their lives are like, and they couldn't ever dream of ours.

Sarah, Zeeland, Mich.

Perhaps "the school of hard knocks" imparts valuable lessons, but too often its students never graduate.

Warren, 38, Schererville, Ind.

We found:

People from old money can be more insulated from "reality" than the nouveau riche – folks who've recently come into the green by hard work, says Florida psychologist Gary Buffone (gbuffone.blogspot.com), author of "Choking on the Silver Spoon."

"Research shows there are a lot of millionaires and you'd never recognize them – they drive older autos, they're not in mansions – because a lot of their wealth is earned, not given. So they came through life much like the average Joe ... they struggled, worked hard and saved to get where they are."

Moneyed parents can fall into the trap of wanting a better life for their kids and then overprotecting them, he said.

"They keep them in private schools, don't expose them to a broader cross-section of the populace, provide for all their needs, buy their cars and clothes for them."

The privileged life doesn't always add up to the good life, he noted.

"I had a client who inherited millions. Until then he was hard-working, your typical kid. But it turned his life upside-down. He couldn't stay in college, didn't stick with a job, because he didn't have to. It can rob an adult kid of motivation and lead to depression. There's a darker side."

29

No fasting for fast-food workers

They asked:

It seems like every time I go to McDonald's or Wendy's, the workers are fat. Why is this?

Logan, 15, male, Orange Park

You said:

Just a theory: They can't afford to eat healthier, lower-fat diets. Adults working in fast-food establishments probably aren't at the top of the wage scale, and it's been noted before that healthier diets are relatively more expensive. I'd imagine you'll see the same thing in other relatively low-wage jobs.

Cari, female, Austin, Texas

A lot of adults and kids are fat. Fast-food franchises pull their workers from the general population, so it stands to reason that a lot of their workers will be fat. I'm not sure if you're trying to make some causal connection or bizarre political statement, but I'd bet most fat fast-food workers were fat before they started working there.

A., Missouri

We found:

Margo Wootan, director of Nutrition Policy at the Center for Science in the Public Interest in Washington (cspinet.org), was featured liberally in "Super Size Me," Morgan Spurlock's film documenting the nasty health effects of his 30-day exclusive McDonald's diet. (For those who haven't seen it, Spurlock suffered terribly during filming and even lost his lunch on camera after a harrowing try at scarfing another Double Quarter Pounder, Supersize fries and Supersize drink.)

According to Wootan, there doesn't appear to be any published data verifying whether fast-food workers are fatter or thinner than the general population.

Because people tend to think of fast food as unhealthy, "He [Logan] may be projecting on the workers that they are unhealthy. ... Does he have the same impression of wait staff at sit-down restaurants? The amount of calories and fat at sit-downs is actually higher than at fast-food places because the portions are bigger. A sit-down burger can be 900 calories, vs. 300 at a fast-food place."

While one might reasonably assume many fast-food workers are in lower-income brackets, the relationship between obesity and income is "not that straightforward," Wootan said. Low-income women, for example, have been found to be more overweight on average than higher-income women, but it's the opposite for low- and high-income men.

Minding calories while surrounded by cheese-fries or chalupas can't be easy, she said, but fast-food workers ought to bring their own lunch to work when possible.

"And watch out for liquid calories. ... There are six or seven teaspoons of sugar in a glass of presweetened tea. My husband drank fountain soda where he worked. Once I talked him into switching his diet, he lost 10 pounds."

On the street, and out of sight

They asked:

Why don't people view the homeless as "real" people? I was homeless by choice for years, and the rudeness I had to deal with was insane. I would try to ask the time and be told, "No, I don't have any."

Margaret M., 21, Greensboro, N.C.

You said:

I've always viewed the homeless as human beings and nothing less. But many people feel the world revolves around them or that they are better than everyone else. It hurts me to see people homeless, whether by choice or not.

Jes, 20, female, Morgantown, Pa.

Anxious to get away from possibly being accosted or verbally assaulted, most people tend to be curt out of fear.

Frank, 56, Fort Lauderdale

Ninety-nine times out of 100, when a homeless person approaches me, it's to beg for money. They usually smell bad and may be dirty. They also have higher rates of such diseases as tuberculosis. They are more likely to be mentally ill. Having worked in a homeless shelter, I've learned the majority are able-bodied and have chosen a life of substance abuse over self-reliance. Most are out to manipulate the system to get everything they can without being responsible. People realize this and resent them. We're trying to have a society here!

Rick, Springfield, Ohio

Imagine what this world would be like if everyone treated others with love and respect, regardless of their fortunes or misfortunes, cultural differences and beliefs.

Pam, Greenville, Miss.

We found:

Most people who fear the homeless are harboring a stereotype and should get to know them, says Michael Stoops, director of community organizing at the National Coalition for the Homeless (nationalhomeless.org). Besides, giving a homeless person a buck won't upset the fragile socioeconomic balance of our culture.

"Giving directly to the homeless keeps us in touch with the fact that not everyone is doing well," he said. "We're not talking about giving a couple hundred dollars to someone who's going to go buy a 40-ouncer. How can you get yourself in trouble with a dollar?"

Still, the most common public reaction is to ignore the homeless, Stoops said.

"When someone walks by and doesn't acknowledge your existence, it's a form of existential blindness. The person knows that could be them, but ignoring a person and making judgments makes them feel superior."

Americans don't brush off homelessness in general, however. An Associated Press poll found 90 percent consider it a serious problem. And 56 percent said in the long term it's brought on by circumstances beyond a person's control.

But harassment and even killings of the homeless do occur. They are one of the last groups with whom abuse is fair game, Stoops noted. He pointed to the Bumfights video series, in which the homeless were filmed and paid to hurt themselves, and "Bumvertising," which paid Seattle street people to hold placards touting a poker Web site, as examples of exploitation.

Does lots of money equal lots of respect?

They asked:

Why does it seem that people are treated better in almost every aspect if they have plenty of money, while middle-class and lower-class people suffer?

Jaymar, 38, middle class, Lexington, S.C.

You said:

Would you be quicker to do a big favor for your destitute brother-in-law or for Bill Gates?

Morpheus, New York, N.Y.

I don't see great differences in how people are treated. The difference is in who people spend time with. The wealthy do things that aren't available to me because I cannot afford them. On the other hand, the wealthy might prefer being at their yacht club to being in my dining room playing pinochle.

Pete, 43, lower middle class, Livonia, Mich.

I treat all people with dignity. You are the person you are, and money will not change that. If you speak with respect, you will receive respect.

M. Francis, 48, upper middle class, Nevada

People of "higher class" are not always treated better. I've got a job and have never stolen anything in my life, but because I'm a teenager, store clerks automatically look like they need to bolt things down to the counter with a nail gun when I walk in the door.

Ashley, 17, upper middle class, Pasco, Wash.

At some level we probably see the successful as tight with God and hence entitled to extra respect. That attitude is wrong.

Hollis H., 66, middle class, Kansas City, Mo.

We found:

Jim O'Donnell made a tidy sum catering to the rich as head of Fidelity Investments' "High Net Worth" group in Boston. Then he ditched it all, became an economics professor at Huntington College (huntington.edu) in Indiana and wrote books like "Letters for Lizzie" (lettersforlizzie.com) about how faith helped him face his wife's cancer battle.

"It got to a point where I asked myself ... do I want my life to be about helping rich people become richer?"

He didn't leave without forming strong opinions on why the astoundingly affluent regularly get perks.

"We live in a culture increasingly driven by money and celebrity. We think, 'They don't have my problems and if they do, they'll be settled because they understand what moves the world' – money."

Though we may say we envy or dislike the rich, we're actually dying to please them. And not just because they can pay more.

"We've moved away from valuing courage, character, virtue as emblems of what the good life is," O'Donnell said. "Those [qualities] have a small currency value but being on Survivor, now that's 'real' life ... It is now deeply embedded in our culture that wealth and some kind of celebrity has its privileges, and we accept it because we think they are 'better' people."

Take some solace, though: mega-rich people are generally only a bit happier than average folks, according to University of Illinois psychologist Ed Diener. Once money provides basics such as food and shelter, its cache in the "well-being" department drops off considerably, he found in surveys of Forbes' list of richest Americans.

The O.U.T.L.O.U.D.
Method to Dialogue

OPEN UP: This is mostly about opening up to yourself. Why do you want to engage someone? Is it for the right reasons? The answers might help you figure out how to approach another person. A friend once told me the real reason I started Y? wasn't for me to learn more about "Buddhists in Asia or lesbians in San Francisco," but because I wanted to learn something more about myself. He was right. Acknowledging that has helped give me perspective when considering others' answers.

USE YOUR HEAD: Plan for the right question. Not all questions need to be the "wet dogs" variety. Stereotypes and clichés don't work as well as sincere attempts to talk.

TIME IT RIGHT: Create the "O.U.T.L.O.U.D. Moment". Pick your spots for provocative dialogue. Find a genuine opening rather than create a false one. It's often during those down times between all the "vital" discourse that we can most easily find a direct path to someone's point of view. If you spend enough time sitting in the cubicle next to someone of a different culture, chances are there'll come a time — over food, perhaps, or during a power outage — when the topic you've been dying to broach will wend its way naturally into the discussion.

LOCK IN ON THE TARGET: Keeping things simple can give the best chance for getting another's trust and a meaningful reply. Some of the best questions at Y?, those that prompt the most telling answers, are also often the easiest to digest. Remember, it's not about winning your point. It's what comes from the heart that counts most — and captures people's interest. Talking from the heart also means easing into things by letting someone know *why* it would help you to learn the answer to your question before you ask it.

OWN UP TO ASSUMPTIONS: One of the most refreshing and repetitive surprises of the Y? project is the difficulty in predicting how a person will respond to a question. Blacks do not think in lockstep. Nor do whites. Nor Christians or Muslims. Nor gays or straights. Be receptive to another's ideas. Wipe the slate clean and listen to the content of the message, not the color or culture of the messenger.

UNLOAD YOUR EXPECTATIONS: Many of us are thinner-skinned than we'll admit. When we get hit with an answer or comment we hadn't anticipated, our emotions can often get caught off-balance, and our egos get bruised. The solution: Expect the unexpected. You'll never be blindsided or taken aback by information that doesn't gibe with your worldview.

DIGEST THE DIALOGUE: Learning about others doesn't stop when the talking's over. Assess what you're told and how it fits with or departs from your perspectives. Recap your discussion with a third party to distill the most relevant information into its most meaningful points.

ABOUT THE AUTHOR

Phillip J. Milano is the founder of Y? The National Forum on People's Differences, the acclaimed cross-cultural dialogue project that encourages people to ask unflinching, politically incorrect questions about our differences.

Since its creation in 1998, Phillip's web site, YForum.com, has attracted millions of visitors and thousands of questions and answers. He has been featured on CBS, CNN, BET and the BBC, and in numerous newspapers, including The Washington Post, New York Times and USA Today.

He is the author of the Perigee book "I Can't Believe You Asked That!" as well as writer of the pioneering newspaper column/blog "Dare to Ask."

Mr. Milano is a 25-year newspaper veteran. He received his Master of Business Administration from Northern Illinois University and his Bachelor of Science in Journalism from Southern Illinois University.

SPEECHES AND APPEARANCES

Mr. Milano is an in-demand speaker. For bookings, contact

Contemporary Issues Agency
809 Turnberry Drive, Waunakee, WI 53597-2256
Phone: 800-843-2179
Fax: 608-849-6311
www.CIAspeakers.com
Info@CIAspeakers.com